First Grade Puzzles

Word Games, Puzzles and Phonics Fun

Speedy Publishing LLC
40 E. Main St. #1156
Newark, DE 19711
www.speedypublishing.com

Puzzle: Cut & Paste

For cutting purposes

Puzzle: Cut & Paste

For cutting purposes

Puzzle: Cut & Paste

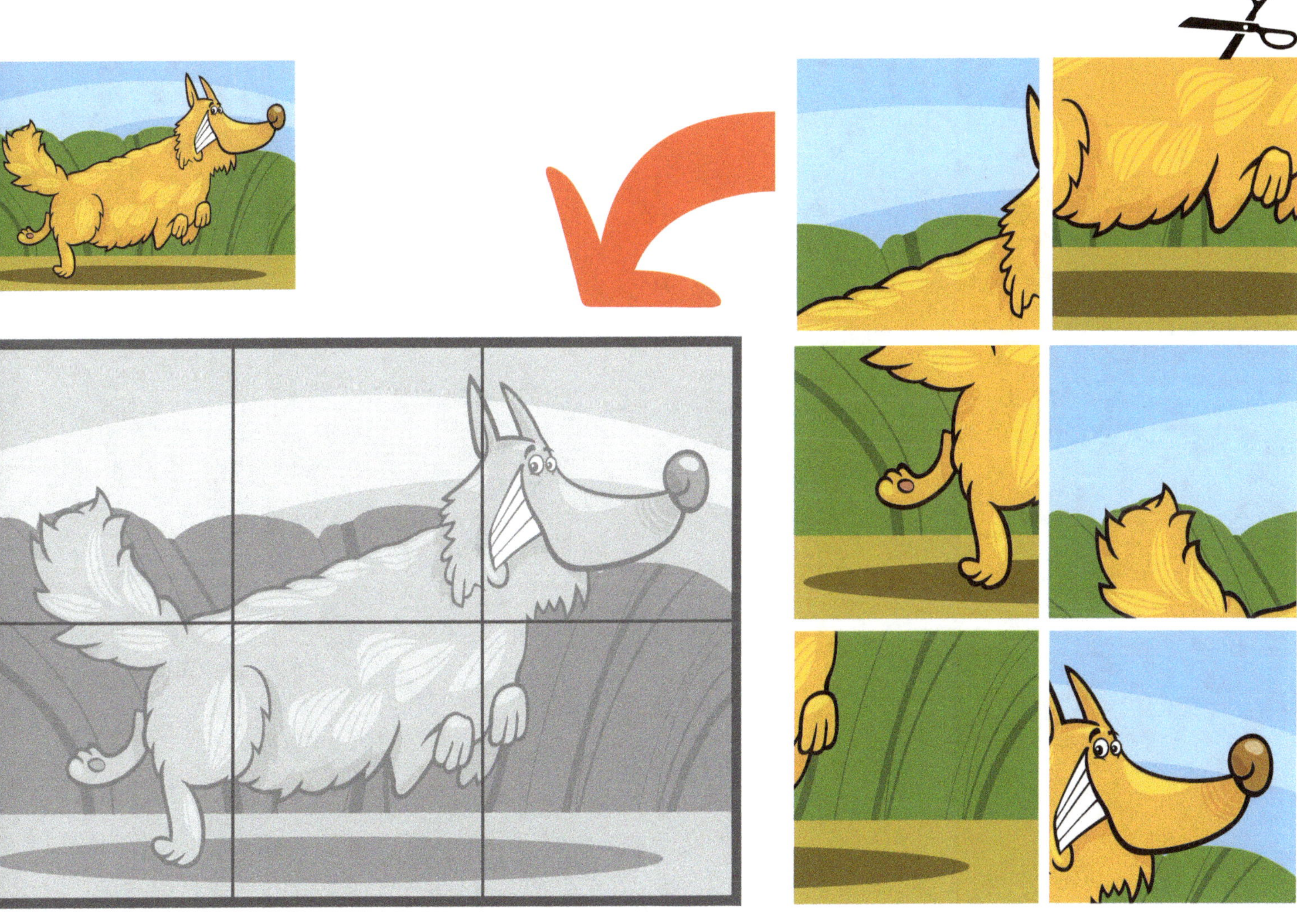

For cutting purposes

Puzzle: Cut & Paste

For cutting purposes

Puzzle: Cut & Paste

For cutting purposes

Puzzle: Cut & Paste

For cutting purposes

Puzzle: Cut & Paste

For cutting purposes

Puzzle: Cut & Paste

For cutting purposes

Puzzle: Cut & Paste

For cutting purposes

Puzzle: Cut & Paste

For cutting purposes

Zigzag Word Seach Puzzle

Family

P	T	S	I	S	T	H	U	N	E
A	N	R	E	T	O	E	N	E	R
R	E	O	M	B	R	R	C	L	D
F	D	T	L	E	R	C	H	I	L
A	N	H	A	T	I	V	S	O	N
T	A	E	R	F	A	E	A	U	N
H	R	N	E	P	T	H	E	R	T
E	G	W	E	H	N	I	E	C	E
R	G	R	A	N	D	D	A	U	G
R	E	H	T	O	M	R	E	T	H

Find all the words from the word list (ignore spaces and dashes):

AUNT
BROTHER
CHILDREN
DAUGHTER
FATHER
GRANDFATHER
GRANDMOTHER
MOTHER
NEPHEW
NIECE
PARENT
RELATIVE
SISTER
SON
UNCLE

Beach

S	U	N	B	A	T	L	A	O	C
C	R	G	N	I	H	L	N	A	E
B	A	U	M	B	R	E	L	A	V
M	I	W	S	A	S	S	L	B	O
M	I	N	G	N	D	E	A	Y	L
L	E	T	O	L	S	E	S	E	L
B	P	F	W	L	U	G	S	T	S
B	I	L	E	L	G	L	A	I	W
E	L	O	S	U	N	E	G	U	I
P	F	P	S	L	O	U	N	S	M

Find all the words from the word list (ignore spaces and dashes):

CRAB
FLIP-FLOPS
GULL
LOUNGE
OCEAN
PEBBLE
SAND
SEA
SUNBATHING
SUNGLASSES
SWIMMING
SWIMSUIT
TOWEL
UMBRELLA
VOLLEYBALL

Flowers

C	W	E	R	A	C	B	L	U	E
O	O	R	N	A	T	L	L	E	B
R	L	L	I	P	I	O	N	D	A
N	F	U	T	A	D	R	Y	A	I
F	P	A	N	I	S	H	S	H	L
O	T	Y	S	Y	Y	C	A	N	T
R	O	E	L	L	M	U	M	E	H
G	N	E	V	A	G	L	A	D	I
E	E	H	T	F	O	S	U	L	O
T	M	L	I	L	Y	R	O	S	E

Find all the words from the word list (ignore spaces and dashes):

BLUEBELL
CARNATION
CHRYSANTHEMUM
CORNFLOWER
DAHLIA
DAISY
FORGET-ME-NOT
GLADIOLUS
LILY OF THE VALLEY
PANSY
ROSE
TULIP

Circus

B	I	G	A	G	Y	M	N	A	S
P	O	T	C	R	O	B	A	T	T
G	U	J	A	M	R	I	N	G	M
G	U	E	G	C	R	E	T	S	A
L	N	L	I	L	N	T	I	C	K
E	I	C	C	O	W	E	L	K	E
R	C	Y	I	A	N	S	A	E	T
T	R	A	P	H	O	R	W	R	F
P	A	R	E	R	O	P	E	K	U
E	D	A	Z	E	T	R	I	C	N

Find all the words from the word list:

ACROBAT
BIG TOP
CLOWN
FUN
GYMNAST
HORSE
JUGGLER
MAGICIAN
PARADE
RINGMASTER
ROPE WALKER
TICKET
TRAPEZE
TRICK
UNICYCLE

Patterns

B	O	H	E	I	R	T	S	T	O
N	A	I	M	P	E	S	P	O	I
E	V	R	A	R	G	Y	L	L	L
H	D	O	G	P	T	A	E	K	E
C	A	N	I	L	A	R	T	A	N
A	M	Y	N	G	I	D	A	D	I
S	P	E	D	H	A	M	N	O	U
K	A	L	O	F	L	H	S	T	Q
H	I	S	G	L	A	A	R	L	E
T	O	O	T	O	R	I	K	A	T

Find all the words from the word list (ignore spaces and dashes):

ARGYLE
BOHEMIAN
CHEVRON
DAMASK
DOGTOOTH
FLORAL
GINGHAM
HARLEQUIN
IKAT
PAISLEY
PLAID
POLKA DOTS
STRIPES
TARTAN
TOILE

Trees

B	E	D	E	U	C	A	L	P	E
I	C	A	S	U	T	P	Y	I	N
R	C	R	O	R	N	B	E	A	M
B	H	A	H	L	D	E	R	D	N
A	N	S	T	A	K	C	E	E	I
B	E	P	U	O	A	H	L	N	L
O	A	B	N	T	S	E	M	P	O
B	P	A	L	M	T	R	E	E	P
E	F	I	R	E	L	P	A	M	L
E	C	H	L	A	R	C	H	R	A

Find all the words from the word list (ignore spaces and dashes):

ALDER	FIR
ASPEN	HORNBEAM
BAOBAB	LARCH
BEECH	LINDEN
BIRCH	MAPLE
CEDAR	OAK
CHESTNUT	PALM TREE
ELM	PINE
EUCALYPTUS	POPLAR

Winter

B	D	E	T	S	O	R	F	S	C
A	S	C	N	E	W	Y	F	R	A
R	E	E	J	R	A	E	M	I	T
E	E	M	A	S	N	O	W	M	T
T	R	B	N	U	A	S	N	A	E
I	T	E	I	S	R	N	E	I	N
N	A	R	C	K	Y	O	L	C	S
G	K	S	E	I	F	W	C	I	H
F	E	B	R	I	L	A	S	L	G
Y	R	A	U	N	G	K	E	E	I

Find all the words from the word list (ignore spaces and dashes):

BARE TREES	MITTENS
DECEMBER	NEW YEAR
FEBRUARY	SCARF
FROST	SKIING
ICE SKATING	SLEIGH
ICICLE	SNOWFLAKE
JANUARY	SNOWMAN

Car Parts

B	R	I	G	H	T	S	T	I	R
U	E	L	O	I	D	A	R	S	E
M	P	D	R	S	P	E	E	D	L
H	E	A	O	N	E	D	O	O	E
R	E	P	O	G	I	N	O	M	E
T	W	I	F	I	W	E	R	E	H
R	U	N	K	N	D	O	W	T	W
L	I	C	E	N	S	E	P	E	G
S	E	A	T	E	T	A	L	R	N
T	L	E	B	S	T	E	E	R	I

Find all the words from the word list
(ignore spaces and dashes):

BUMPER
DOOR
ENGINE
HEADLIGHTS
LICENSE PLATE
RADIO
ROOF
SEAT BELT
SPEEDOMETER
STEERING WHEEL
TIRES
TRUNK
WINDOW
WIPER

www.ingramcontent.com/pod-product-compliance
Lightning Source LLC
LaVergne TN
LVHW060832170826
845678LV00010B/1963

9798869449023